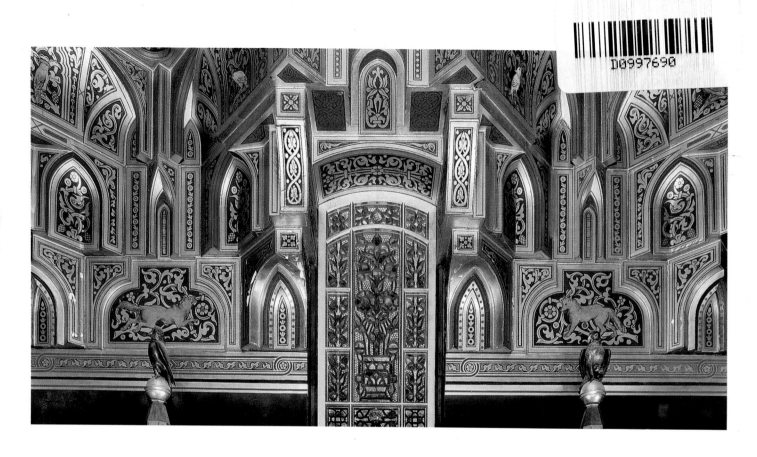

The essential CARDIFF CASTLE

MATTHEW WILLIAMS

Contents

In the Beginning: the Romans

The castle stands at the lowest crossing point of the River Taff, near the mouth of the Bristol Channel. Little is known about life in the area before the Roman invasion of 43AD. The local tribe was the Silures, who farmed the land and may have been descendants of a long-established pre-Celtic civilization. The Roman historian Tacitus describes them as having dark complexions and curly hair.

The forces of the invading Roman army soon reached what is now south-east Wales. By the end of the 40s, the area was coming increasingly under the influence of the Roman military, followed by a civilian administration.

By 51AD, the stubborn resistance put up by the Silures had been gradually defeated. The key to successful Roman occupation involved a process of Romanisation which nevertheless retained elements of the local culture. In time, even the warlike Silures yielded to this policy, witnessing improved trade and communication as well as the efficient administrative and judicial system that the Romans introduced.

ABOVE AND RIGHT: Roman shields served to protect most of a soldier's body.

FAR RIGHT: The outer faces of the walls were built of cut blocks of local blue lias limestone, with a very substantial core of large boulders, probably taken from the bed of the River Taff. These boulders are set in extremely durable cement, giving the wall great solidity and strength. Against the wall was an earth bank, excavated from the outer ditch and providing access to the top of the wall.

CARDIFF: A REMOTE CORNER OF THE ROMAN EMPIRE

The Roman fort at Cardiff was probably established at the end of the 50s, on a strategic site that afforded easy access to the sea. The sea was both a defence and a vital means of communication, and Cardiff could become a naval base if required.

Archaeological excavations made during the 1970s indicated that this was only the first of four different forts, each a different size, that occupied the present site. All four conformed to the roughly square shape that the Romans favoured. The first fort, which was presumably intended to subdue the population following the initial invasion, was the largest, extending to some 12 hectares. The second and third forts were smaller, being part of a system of garrisons rather than a frontier station.

Unlike the three earlier wooden versions, the final Roman fort, built in the fourth century, had walls of stone. This fourth fort was heavily defended, as by this time the Roman Empire was under attack.

Following the fall of the Roman Empire, the country became a series of small kingdoms and the Welsh identity began to take shape. Christianity pervaded Wales but on the whole the period is cloaked in obscurity. It seems likely that the Roman fort at Cardiff was virtually abandoned, but the settlement established outside its walls remained, eventually becoming the modern city of Cardiff.

RIGHT: Archaeology can tell us a great deal about how the Romans lived in Cardiff two thousand years ago. Pots have been excavated that were originally imported from all over the Roman Empire. These vessels once held oils and wines, giving us clues about the Roman diet.

BELOW: Inside the stone fort, there would have been a number of wooden buildings associated with the requirements of the garrison. These probably included a Commander's house, barrack buildings and stabling. A bathhouse probably stood in the south-western corner of the site, where the remains of a hypocaust or central heating pipe were discovered. Immediately outside the walls of the fort were shops that would have supplied the needs of the garrison.

ABOVE: The remains of the north gate of the Roman fort were uncovered amid great excitement in 1899. This contemporary photograph shows one of two guard chambers which originally stood at the base of two tall towers which looked out to the north.

OPPOSITE LEFT: The gate to the Roman fort, with its two towers, was reconstructed twice, first in about 1905 by Lord Bute's architect William Frame, and again in 1922.

LEFT: The reconstructed Roman walls; Lord Bute ordered that the original stonework should be clearly identified by being outlined in red sandstone.

THE ROMANS RE-DISCOVERED

For nearly 900 years, Cardiff Castle's Roman past remained hidden and forgotten beneath banks of earth added by the Normans. Its Roman origins were only discovered in 1888, when the 3rd Marquess of Bute decided to build a new tower on the east bank of the castle and to extend the grounds. Bute's workmen began to tunnel through what was assumed to be a solid earth bank; to their astonishment the substantial remains of Roman stonework appeared, and the history of the castle was pushed back by hundreds of years.

Lord Bute decided to abandon his original plans, and to investigate and reconstruct the Roman fort instead. He ordered that the outside of the earth bank on the east of the castle be cut away, so as to expose the full extent of the remains, and from 1897 the walls were gradually rebuilt on their original foundations.

Lord Bute's decision to reconstruct the Roman fort was unprecedented; Cardiff Castle is the only place in Britain where such an ambitious undertaking has been attempted, thanks to Bute's enthusiasm as a rich and scholarly patron.

The Roman walls were reconstructed in what was thought at the time to be an accurate way, with one exception, the addition of a gallery within them. This was built for two reasons: to allow access to the substantial lower level of Roman remains; and so that Lord Bute could still take his daily exercise even in bad weather.

The Roman wall galleries found a new role during World War II, when they were used as air-raid shelters by shoppers and cinema-goers from busy nearby streets during enemy action, accommodating nearly 2000 people.

ABOVE: This late nineteenth-century photograph shows Lord Bute's men working on the excavation of the Roman wall.

BELOW: Lord Bute had a passage built inside the reconstructed wall to act as a viewing gallery.

The Normans:
A Struggle for Power

In 1066 the Normans marched into southern England and in 1067 William of Normandy was crowned king. He went on to conquer south-east Wales, founding a castle in Cardiff in 1081, and by 1093 Robert Fitzhamon was established as Earl of Gloucester and Lord of Glamorgan. Over the next 30 years the Normans gradually destroyed many of the ancient Welsh kingdoms, although their control was always firmest in Monmouthshire and Glamorgan.

They also re-used the site of the fourth-century Roman fort. The stone outer walls had probably survived only in part, but the defensive earth banks and ditches were now massively enlarged and reinforced by the new occupiers. The site was divided into inner and outer wards, separated by a huge stone wall, the remains of which can still be seen dividing the Green. In the inner ward, at the heart of the new castle, the Normans created a motte, or artificial hill, to allow them to defend the castle effectively from a high vantage point.

The first keep on the motte was erected by Fitzhamon and, along with many of these early defences, was probably built of wood, as any stone building built upon the new motte would have been unstable. Fitzhamon's daughter, Mabel, married the second Norman lord of the castle, known as Robert the Consul, and it was he who replaced the wooden keep with a stone version, probably in response to a Welsh uprising in 1135. The new stone keep, and the water-filled moat around the motte, made a successful attack even more difficult.

Over the next two centuries the castle was owned by successive powerful families, including the de Clares, the Despensers and the Beauchamps. Each added further fortifications to the site, and the keep was linked by a large and well-defended wall to the Black Tower, which had been built at the gate.

ABOVE: Cardiff Castle was for centuries the seat of royal and administrative power in the county of Glamorgan.

LEFT: All that remains of the great wall separating the inner and outer wards.

OPPOSITE: Robert of Normandy, the eldest son of King William the Conqueror, was held prisoner by his nephew Robert the Consul at the castle. William Burges' design for the mantelpiece in the Banqueting Hall shows Robert the Consul on horseback, and his prisoner languishing behind bars.

ROBERTVS CONSVL COM̃ GLŌ

THE KEEP

The twelve-sided keep at Cardiff is the finest in Wales, and is built of blue lias limestone. It is of a type known as a 'shell' keep; its outer walls provided a shell for smaller buildings within it. It was intended to provide accommodation for the lord and his household and was always the most secure and well fortified part of the medieval castle. It had its own well and could be heavily provisioned against a siege.

Despite being more securely built in stone and surrounded by a moat, it could still be vulnerable to attack. One of the most famous incidents in the castle's history took place during a night raid in 1158, when the Welsh leader Ifor Bach scaled the walls of the keep and abducted the Earl, his wife and their infant son. He held them to ransom until he had secured the return of land to which he was entitled under Welsh law.

LEFT: By the eighteenth century the keep was a complete ruin. When this view was painted in 1789, there was a plan, never executed, to install a domed copper roof and turn it into 'a dancing room'.

OPPOSITE LEFT: The keep has had various names over the centuries, such as Iestyn's Tower and the White Tower. It has also been considerably altered and is now much smaller than it once was. A large Great Hall inside the 'shell' was destroyed in the 1640s during the Civil War, and the massive fore-buildings that extended down the motte were demolished by 1784.

From Fortress to Mansion

In 1404 the Welsh hero Owain Glyndŵr attacked Cardiff, destroying the town and severely damaging the castle. Following Owain's eventual defeat, the castle was repaired, and a new residential block was begun on the west of the site during the 1420s and 1430s, when the castle was owned by Richard Beauchamp, Earl of Warwick.

A powerful and important figure, Beauchamp built himself a more comfortable and less fortified residence than the by now somewhat old-fashioned keep. His new mansion contained a Great Hall, as well as private accommodation for the lord and his family.

The castle reverted to the crown at the end of the fifteenth century and remained in royal hands until Edward VI granted it to William Herbert, 1st Earl of Pembroke, in 1551. Wilton House in Wiltshire was the family's main residence, but the 2nd Earl spent more time at Cardiff than his father. During the 1570s he 'translated and repaired all the rooms of the castle', adding a new tower on the south of the house, and moving his private chambers into a large new north wing. He also modernised the keep and the Black Tower and created a new private garden, 'the Lord's Plaisance' beneath the Ladies' Walk.

ABOVE: William Herbert, 1st Earl of Pembroke, who was granted Cardiff Castle by King Edward VI in 1551.

LEFT: The 'Ladies' Walk' provided a safe and comfortable place for ladies to take exercise. Although much of the stonework is medieval, the core of the wall is Roman. The walk overlooked the, probably elaborate, gardens laid out by the 2nd Earl of Pembroke around 1570.

The interior of the house in the 1580s was filled with rich furnishings such as silks and tapestries. This reflected the standing of its owners, Lord and Lady Pembroke, who were important figures at the Tudor Court, favourites of Queen Elizabeth I and patrons of literature and the arts.

The Earls of Pembroke, although largely absent, were lords of the castle until the late seventeenth century. During the Civil War, the 4th Earl sided with Parliament and his castle was seized by the Royalists; it suffered severe damage, particularly to the keep, which was never again occupied as a residence.

LEFT: As the threat of attack declined, the keep became of secondary importance as a residence for the Lord and his family. The mansion built in the 1420s and 30s was more modern and comfortable.

RIGHT: The mansion as it appears today, largely due to the alterations made by the Bute family. Although they visited the castle for only for a few weeks each year, a huge amount of time and money was lavished on alterations.

OPPOSITE: This view from the keep painted in 1789 shows the dramatic changes made by 'Capability' Brown. He demolished ancient walls and gates, as well as the medieval chapel and Shire Hall on the Castle Green.

BELOW: The Butes acquired Cardiff Castle through marriage in 1776. An ancient family who traced their roots back to the kings of Scotland, the Butes made a vast fortune from coal mined on their Welsh estates.

ARRIVAL OF THE BUTES

In 1683 Charlotte Herbert inherited the castle and its Glamorganshire estate from her father, the 7th Earl of Pembroke, and it was her grand-daughter who, in 1766, married the 1st Marquess of Bute.

In the next 30 years the Bute family completely transformed the castle. The 1st Marquess was created Baron Cardiff of Cardiff Castle in 1776, and he and his wife employed the architect Henry Holland and the renowned landscape designer 'Capability' Brown for a major overhaul of the castle, which had been neglected since the Civil War. New wings were added to the house in a Georgian 'Gothick' style, and substantial alterations were made to the interior.

The Castle Green witnessed the most dramatic changes. Capability Brown demolished the massive ward wall that divided the site into inner and outer wards. He also swept away ancient and important buildings that were in the way of his and Bute's vision of a fashionable landscape setting for the house. The keep, shorn of its fore-buildings, was now left isolated on the motte, and Bute attracted much criticism for his lack of appreciation for the castle's ancient character. He also tried to remove houses and workshops that fringed the castle's outer walls, but he had only limited success with this, and the task was finally completed by his great great grandson in the 1920s.

The Victorian Castle

The Bute family first rebuilt the mansion in the 1770s, but it was the Victorian alterations of the 3rd Marquess and his architect William Burges that make Cardiff Castle an extraordinary and outstanding example of Gothic Revival architecture. Their joint vision created a feudal extravaganza of painted murals, stained glass, gilding and sculpture, all set within the framework of the Norman castle turned mansion.

LEFT: The ceiling of the Winter Smoking Room is decorated with murals designed by William Burges and painted by the artist Fred Weekes. These signs of the zodiac were inspired by medieval decoration, and held a great fascination for both Lord Bute and Burges.

BELOW: Burges wrote that 'a keen sense of the comic is generally found in most superior men'. His designs are rich with puns, jokes and medieval-style grotesques, such as this one representing the metal 'Lead'.

The architect William Burges' most memorable work was here in Wales, for his most important client, the 3rd Marquess of Bute. Lord Bute was only 18 and Burges 20 years older when they were introduced in Cardiff in 1865. It was truly a meeting of minds; Lord Bute called his friend 'the soul-inspiring Burges'. Both men were intelligent and imaginative and both were fascinated by the world of the Middle Ages. The result of their collaboration is truly unique.

Burges was quoted as saying that if we want to know what the Middle Ages were like, then we must go to the east. Several interiors at the castle reflect this taste for colour and exoticism. During the summer months, the Butes travelled throughout Europe and the Near East. Together with Burges they would seek new ideas for the castle, such as the glorious gilded ceiling of the Arab Room, or the Roman style of the Roof Garden.

OPPOSITE: Much of the stonework in the castle was carved by the London sculptor Thomas Nicholls, and then painted and decorated. These nearly life-sized figures represent two of the eight winds of classical antiquity.

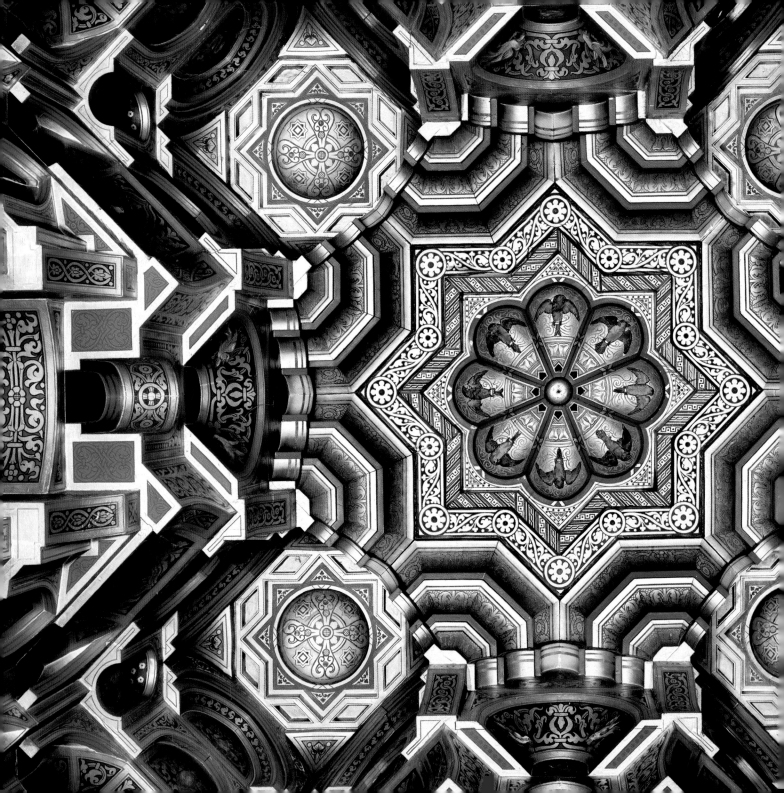

LEFT: The ceiling of the Arab Room is one of the glories of the castle. Known as a *muquarnas* ceiling, it is made of wood and covered with pure gold-leaf. The Arab Room was commissioned shortly before Burges' death in 1881.

RIGHT: A taste for the exotic pervades the castle interior; the Roof Garden at the top of the Bute Tower dates from 1875 and was inspired by Roman discoveries at Pompeii.

RIGHT: Bronze beavers play on the fountain of the Roof Garden. Lord Bute brought real beavers into the castle grounds in 1873; his plan was to re-introduce species that had once been common in medieval Britain.

CRAFTSMANSHIP

ABOVE: The talented men of the Bute workshops produced some exquisite carvings throughout the castle, using walnut, teak and oak.

RIGHT: This gloriously colourful stained glass dragon is derived from ancient legend; it was made by Charles Campbell in 1884.

BELOW: William Burges kept a controlling hand on his creative projects. His team of craftsmen, although many of them were his friends, had to adhere strictly to his designs.

Burges had already worked on several restoration projects by the time he met Lord Bute, and had begun to gather a 'team' of sculptors, stained glass makers and other craftsmen who were aware of Burges' interest in reviving medieval techniques. These craftsmen worked with Burges on other successful projects, such as his major commission for re-building Cork Cathedral in Ireland and a country house project, Knightshayes Court in Devonshire.

The re-building of Cardiff Castle caused a burst of creativity. Bute and Burges surrounded themselves with artists and craftsmen who could make their dreams a reality. As well as Burges' favourite team of artists and sculptors, local craftsmen who had completed the restoration of nearby Llandaff Cathedral now also came to the castle.

In the Cardiff docks, a talented group of woodcarvers and joiners gathered to form the 'Bute workshops'. This team of some 20 craftsmen worked for many years at the castle, and also on Lord Bute's various other building projects in Wales, England and Scotland.

The distinguished Welsh sculptor Sir William Goscombe John began his career at the castle, training under his father Thomas. Lord Bute was keen to encourage such talents, and during the 1880s the decorative work at the castle became an inspiration to local style. The new houses of prosperous businessmen, often built on Bute estate land, were similarly decorated with carvings, glass and tiles.

'THE RICHEST BABY IN BRITAIN':
THE 3RD MARQUESS OF BUTE

OPPOSITE: The statue of the Madonna and Child in the Roof Garden dates from 1875–76 and is in medieval French style. Burges designed the figure to be lit by the rays of the setting sun.

BELOW: Sixteen carved wooden angels, holding shields bearing family heraldry, support the Banqueting Hall roof. Burges had seen similar angels in the churches of East Anglia.

The 3rd Marquess of Bute (1847–1900) is usually remembered as a vastly rich and eccentric Roman Catholic. Rich he most certainly was, and a Catholic convert, but he was not an eccentric. Bute was in fact a shy, gentle and scholarly man, whose tastes were for the world of the past, not the industrial world that produced his wealth. Like William Burges, Bute had a passion for history. He was also a linguist, an archaeologist and a mystic, as well as being one of the richest men in the world.

Cardiff Castle was only one of the many homes he inherited from his father, who died when Bute was only a baby. He spent much of his happy childhood at the castle, until his happiness ended with his mother's death when he was 12. He grew into a shy, withdrawn youth, ill at ease in conventional society, and his wealth made him mistrustful of the friendship of others. He drew comfort from his studies and, increasingly, from religion. When he was 21, he converted, amid some scandal, to Roman Catholicism.

Religion was central to Bute's life. He attended daily Mass, and throughout his life was keen to build and restore churches, monasteries or convents on or near his estates, as well as reconstructing his various homes.

Lord Bute was hugely proud of being a Scotsman, but he was also very sympathetic to the Welsh language and Welsh culture. He learned to speak Welsh; he supported the National Eisteddfod, a Welsh cultural festival; and he encouraged Welsh singing and harp playing in the Banqueting Hall when the family were in residence. In so many ways, Bute was a man born out of his own time. Unlike the majority of his contemporaries, he was opposed to blood sports and he also supported the education of women.

TOP: Scholarly, devout and mystical, the 3rd Marquess of Bute was one of the most interesting men of his generation. He died in 1900 of Bright's disease at the early age of 53.

ABOVE: The delicate green marble columns in Lord Bute's bedroom are ornamented with chunky annulets, each carved with a different creature.

LEFT: Lord Bute's bedroom in the Bute Tower is a highly personal space. The decoration has a biblical theme, and the gilt bronze figure of St John the Evangelist dominates the chimneypiece.

A CHILD'S PARADISE

Lord and Lady Bute had four children, Lady Margaret, Lord Dumfries, Lord Ninian and Lord Colum. The children liked coming to Cardiff Castle, which was the most ancient and romantic of the family's homes.

Mornings were spent at their lessons in the Day Nursery. This room is one of Burges' most delightful creations, with tiled decoration illustrating heroes and heroines from children's literature. In the afternoons, the Bute children would ride their ponies, be taken fishing by one of the footmen, or play in the pleasure grounds behind the castle.

ABOVE AND ABOVE RIGHT: The Day Nursery is in the Guest Tower and dates from 1879. Here the Bute children were looked after by their governess, nurse and two nursery maids.

RIGHT: The Bute children, photographed around 1888; they enjoyed a loving relationship with their parents and the Marquess was especially close to his eldest child and only daughter, Margaret.

RIGHT: This ingenious tile design shows the Invisible Prince; his profile, crowned with leaves, emerges above the falcon.

OSAND ◉ DIAMONDS: RED ◉ RIDING ◉ HOOD: ◉ REYNARD:FRIAR

ABOVE: The tiled frieze in the Day Nursery was made in 1879 and depicts a procession of heroes and heroines from children's literature. It was painted by H.W. Lonsdale to Burges' designs and made by Maw & Co.

A WORKING HOUSEHOLD

When the family were in residence the household had an indoor staff of about 20, with a further 20 working in the gardens and stables. Together with staff from the home farm, the head gardener and the six Castle Lodge keepers and their families, these formed a large self-contained community. Even when Lord and Lady Bute were at another of their homes, flowers, peaches and grapes from Cardiff Castle hothouses would be sent to them by train.

The Butes had a reputation for being good employers and servants enjoyed good food and security in return for their extremely hard work. Some servants, such as the butler, footmen and maids, even had the luxury of travelling abroad with the family. When the Butes moved between houses, a train was chartered to accommodate the family, staff, and chests of family silverware.

ABOVE: During the long periods when the family were not in residence, a 'skeleton' staff stayed on at the castle. The group pictured here in 1891 would have kept the house freshly aired in readiness for a visit.

ABOVE: The maids' day began very early in the morning, when they lit the fires. Rooms such as Lord Bute's bathroom were plumbed for hot water but most visitors had hot water carried upstairs by the maids.

RIGHT: Bottles of shampoo and a reviving tonic give a personal touch in Lord Bute's bathroom.

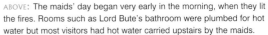

HEAT, LIGHT AND PLUMBING

Although Bute was passionately interested in the world of the past, he was surprisingly keen on modern inventions such as bathrooms, electric light and central heating. He installed electricity in Cardiff Castle as early as 1883, and Burges was happy to incorporate the radiators of the new central heating system into his library tables.

ABOVE: The brightly painted majolica washbasin in Lord Bute's bathroom has no plughole but instead tips up to allow the water to drain. The bowl was designed by William Burges and illustrates Tennyson's poem 'The Mermaid'.

TOP RIGHT: The cellars held wine made at the castle itself between 1875 and 1914. The Bute vineyards were at Castell Coch and on the Glamorganshire coast at Swanbridge.

RIGHT: The decoration of the castle is highly personal to the Bute family; these painted grapevines appear in Lord Bute's own bedroom.

WELSH WINE

Bute was such an ardent medievalist that, having read of the vineyards that once flourished locally during the Middle Ages, he decided to plant vineyards on his Glamorgan estates. In this unique experiment the vines thrived, and for 50 years Welsh wines were produced at Cardiff Castle. The cellars that Bute built and the large oak wine vats installed for storing the new wine are still in place.

The Bute family would invite friends to join them every October for a Welsh 'Vindemia' – an experience that everybody, especially the Bute children, enjoyed.

OPPOSITE FAR RIGHT: Painted gemstones appear on the walls of the Bachelor Bedroom, where the decoration is all on a theme of mineral wealth.

BELOW: The panelled walls of one interior are set with different marbles, each variety named in a gold inscription.

LEFT: The murals on the walls of the Bachelor Bedroom, painted by H.W. Lonsdale, tell the story of man's pursuit of mineral wealth and illustrate stories from Herodotus and Homer.

The Castle Interior: Themes and Influences

Design ideas for the various rooms in the castle probably came from both Burges and Bute, and they drew on many sources for inspiration. In the Banqueting Hall, for instance, scenes from the life of the second Norman lord of the castle dominate the walls and chimneypiece.

MINERAL WEALTH

The enormous wealth that Lord Bute poured into his restorations mostly came from Welsh industry. His father had laid the foundations of this wealth when he built a dock at Cardiff that eventually exported Welsh coal to the rest of the world. The Bute family owned the mineral rights over their 20,000 acres of Glamorganshire land, and a booming export industry greatly expanded the family wealth.

Although Cardiff was at the heart of the commercial boom which enabled Bute to indulge his pleasures, he had very little interest in commerce itself. He did, however, commemorate the source of the family fortune in one of the Clock Tower rooms. The chimneypiece in the Bachelor Bedroom includes specimens of minerals from the Glamorgan estates, and the whole room represents the treasures of the earth. The extraordinary bathroom adjoining the bedroom has a marble bath, and the room is lined with a rich pink local alabaster.

RIGHT: One chimneypiece in the castle is set with specimens of minerals found on the Marquess of Bute's estates in Glamorgan, the source of the family's money.

ABOVE: Lord Bute's bath is said to be a Roman antique. Burges inset metal sea creatures into the surface, which appeared to move when the bath was full. The walls of the bathroom are of a local pink alabaster.

Murals on the walls of the Banqueting Hall tell the story of the medieval castle and echo the style of medieval manuscript illumination. The idea of wall murals was inspired by medieval churches and castles; Burges himself wrote that the walls of his buildings should 'speak and tell a story', just as the painted walls of a medieval church would once have illustrated Bible stories. In 1874, one critic wrote that the wall decoration of Lord Bute's Clock Tower could be read 'like a book'.

CROCODILES, APES AND PEACOCKS

Lord Bute loved animals. As a shy and lonely child, he found great comfort in the company of his pets, especially his beloved dog Mungo and his pet hedgehogs. As an adult, Bute opposed hunting and he forbade his gamekeepers to shoot rabbits around his home on the Isle of Bute.

When he began the restoration of Cardiff Castle, the new decoration included hundreds of animals, birds and insects, in stained glass, carved wood, stone and marquetry. Burges was equally keen on animals and his research into medieval manuscripts revealed the pleasure the Middle Ages also took in both real and imaginary beasts. Burges' designs frequently include eccentric grotesques from his own imagination, as well as more familiar creatures such as parrots and rabbits.

BELOW: The bell push in the Small Dining Room was carved by the Bute workshops, and appropriately takes the form of a 'Howler' monkey, known for its loud scream. The nut in the monkey's mouth could be pressed to summon the steward. A maid could be called by pressing the centre of a carved rose in another part of the oak panelling.

LEFT: Exquisitely carved marquetry birds decorate the bookcases in the Library.

ABOVE: This glorious gilded crocodile lurks on the staircase to startle the unwary, suddenly appearing to those ascending the stair. It dates from the 1880s and was probably carved by Thomas Nicholls.

ABOVE LEFT: There are thousands of animals, birds and insects to be found in the decoration of Cardiff Castle and butterflies are a particular favourite.

LEFT: Based upon a Welsh legend, this carving in the Banqueting Hall shows Prince Llywelyn's faithful dog Gelert, who guards his infant son against a predatory wolf.

The theme of animals extends outside the castle, and the Animal Wall is one of Cardiff's most beloved features. It was also one of Burges' most delightful conceptions, although it was not begun until some years after the architect's death in 1881. The animals were carved by Burges' favourite sculptor, Thomas Nicholls, and the figures were painted in naturalistic colours. This, together with their glass eyes, must have given them a realistic appearance, but the paint weathered badly and was never re-applied. The original group of eight different animals stood directly outside the castle and the lions with shields guarded the main entrance. In the 1920s the wall was moved further to the west, and the 4th Marquess added a further group of six animals, carved by the Scottish sculptor Alexander Carrick.

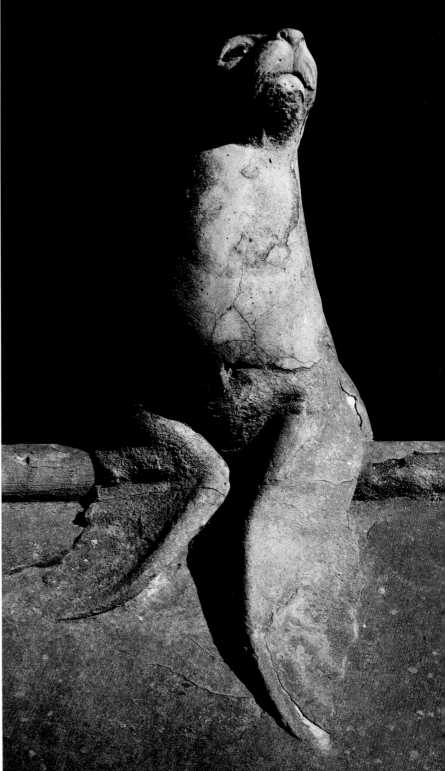

OPPOSITE FAR LEFT: The pair of lions on the Animal Wall bear shields with the Bute arms. The lions, which were carved in London, once flanked the main entrance to the castle.

OPPOSITE: The people of Cardiff have always loved the Animal Wall, and the figures have been immortalised in cartoon strips and in children's fiction over the years.

RIGHT: This tile picture showing the struggle of Hercules and the lion represents 'Leo' in the astrological decoration of the Summer Smoking Room. The panel dates from 1874, and was painted by Frederick Smallfield.

LANGUAGE AND LITERATURE

ABOVE AND TOP RIGHT: The ten library bookcases contain some of the finest marquetry made by the Bute workshops. The three Greek writers Sophocles, Euripides and Aeschylus appear in these end panels, dating from 1879 and reflecting Bute's scholarly interests.

Lord Bute was a highly intelligent and literate man; he had libraries in all his houses, and he also collected rare volumes. The library at Cardiff Castle was created in the space once occupied by the medieval Great Hall and the 'Middle Room'. William Burges turned them into one larger space, making a low-ceilinged and comfortable library for Lord Bute's use. The desks and library tables are original to the room and were designed by Burges.

At Cardiff Castle there are references from classical literature that many educated Victorians would have recognised. The French Gothic spire or flèche was added by William Burges to the fifteenth-century Beauchamp Tower in the late 1870s. The spire itself is made of wood, and covered in elaborately decorated lead. The added height allowed the upper part of the tower to become the Chaucer Room, an extraordinary private sitting room for Lady Bute. Part of the Butes' pleasure in staying at Cardiff Castle was the re-design of individual interiors, and Gwendolen Bute took a particular interest in her own rooms both here and at Castell Coch. The theme of the Chaucer Room decoration may well have been her own choice and was inspired by the English medieval writer Geoffrey Chaucer. The stained glass, murals and sculpture all illustrate his stories.

The stained glass in the Chaucer Room lantern is one of the glories of the castle. The windows illustrate *The Canterbury Tales* and were made by the firm of Saunders and Co, later Worral and Co., around 1880–82. The stained glass maker Gualbert Saunders had worked for William Burges for many years, and Burges encouraged him to set up his own studio. Gualbert was a very talented colourist and his glass can be extraordinarily beautiful. He shared Burges' love of the medieval style, and these panels capture some of Chaucer's exuberance.

RIGHT: The interior of the spire above the Chaucer Room has a kaleidoscopic effect. The room was a private sitting room for Lady Bute, and in later years was used as a guest bedroom.

BELOW: The stained glass of the Chaucer Room can only be truly appreciated close up, but this involves climbing a flight of narrow and dangerous stone stairs, walking a parapet outside the tower, and ducking through a low door into the gallery.

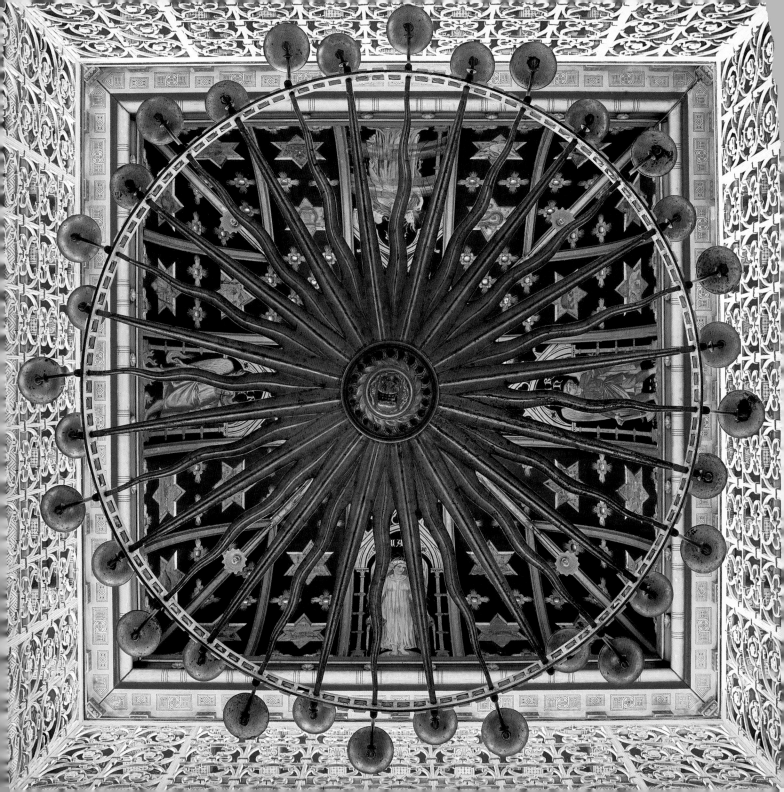

RELIGION, MYSTICISM AND THE 'UNSEEN'

Although he was an extremely devout man and a Catholic convert, Bute nonetheless had a huge interest in the 'unseen'; the paranormal, spiritualism, the occult and astrology all fascinated him.

His friend and architect William Burges had long been interested in astrology, and he may well have passed this interest to Lord Bute. For Bute it became a ruling passion, and his diaries are packed with references to astrology. He regularly consulted astrologers, and attributed disasters to the unfavourable movements of the planets. He even had predictive astrological charts drawn up for his infant children.

Bute's houses reflect his passion, and the castle's Clock Tower in particular is suffused with astrological symbols. Statues of the planets dominate the exterior, and the three interiors Burges designed are all permeated with astrological references. At Mount Stuart, Lord Bute's magnificent home on the Isle of Bute in Scotland, Bute created a Horoscope Room, and its ceiling shows the planets as they were on the day of his own birth.

Bute was also fascinated by the idea of ghosts, and was a member of the Society for Psychical Research. He investigated the paranormal wherever he could, and his academic mind was always drawn to the mystery of the inexplicable.

Into the Modern Age

The 3rd Marquess of Bute died when he was only 53, in 1900. He had transformed the castle into a Welsh Victorian Camelot – now regarded as being of international significance.

Despite huge death duties on the estate, the 4th Marquess completed many of his father's restoration projects, including the reconstruction of the Roman wall. The Bute family continued to stay at Cardiff Castle throughout the 1920s and 30s, although they had sold off many of their business interests in south Wales.

Following the death of the 4th Marquess in 1947, the family decided to present the castle and much of its park as a gift to the City of Cardiff. For 25 years the castle was home to the National College of Music and Drama, and since 1974 it has become one of Wales' most popular tourist attractions.

Cardiff Castle remains a much-loved civic treasure, at the emotional heart of the city that began to grow around the site of its castle two thousand years ago.

LEFT: Now a popular and successful destination, Cardiff Castle amazes its visitors by the extraordinary interiors held within the prickly silhouette of its towers.

ABOVE: In 1947 the Bute family gave the castle to the city of Cardiff as a gift. This munificent legacy has allowed the park to be preserved, providing a splendid setting for the castle itself.